Writings from
Life's Treasure Chest III
Copyright 2016
TXu 2-023-641
All Rights Reserved

Unless otherwise indicated, all scripture quotations are taken from the King James Version of the Bible.

For information contact

William Borum, Jr.
744 Washboard Road
Estill, SC 29918
ISBN: 978-0-9975037-5-3

Preface

In 1991, the World of Poetry, over 1.7 million poets strong (worldwide) presented William an award merit certificate for the poem "A Child's Thoughts". He has received a Golden Poet trophy for the poem "Zeal Where Art Thou" (Changed to 'Lamentation'), and is listed as one of the best new poets of 1988 by the American Poetry Association.

William Borum, affectionately known to his friends as 'Zeke', decided one day, during a spell of illness to write about his life in poetry, prose, and short stories. He was not sure he could write another poem or anything after his first poem, but through perseverance and inspiration, he began writing poem after poem. Then he fell into a dry spell, for lack of a better word, 'the mind went blank'. he would began again. Anyone going through similar struggles and need understanding of how to cope when life takes a turn against you, and If you are determined to make a success after a two year layoff. These writings are intended to help someone like himself who did not live a good family life as a child. Now a mature man in his seventies he looks back remembering his roots and thanking God that the experience made him a better person. He is now happily married and has struggled and sacrificed his life to the Lord Jesus Christ. He is now a leader in the Church of God In Christ. All of his writings point back to his childhood which he has never regretted. These writings are geared to help you with problems in your life.

Table of CONTENT

Writings from Life's Treasure Chest III

A Brother's Love

This episode takes place around the year 1940; about ten months after the beginning of World War II. In a little city of Long Island, called Mosquito Cove. It was early that Sunday morning. Billy had been awake all night. He had gone to a movie, Saturday night, called Stairway to Heaven. It was about dying and ghosts. What he remembered most was the wind blowing the curtains through the window where the ghost made his departure.

1

Everyone in Billy's family went to bed early every night, especially during the cold winter months. That night was a very cold night but the house was very warm.

Toward the end of the room stood a coal stove banked for the night and cherry red. Opposite the coal stove was a brand new kerosene heater, lit to give additional heat. Because heat rises it must have been very warm upstairs, apparently, someone opened the window and forgot to close it.

2

He had been given permission from his parents, to see a movie this night with his friend. After coming into the house and turning out the lights that had been left on until he returned home, he heard his mom call from her bedroom to confirm that he was home and ready to go to bed.

---As Billy was about to ascend the staircase, at the very top, where the hallway began, he noticed a window

3

opened one-quarter the way up from the bottom and the long white cotton curtains that draped it like a flowing gown was floating in a breeze that suddenly came from nowhere. He began rising slowing step-by-step, his eyes fixed on those ghastly-ghostly floating curtains. He finally reached his room. He felt unusually tired from the climbing those stairs. On any given day, he could make that climb with apparent ease.

Before sliding under the warm covers, he remembered to say his prayers. With fear in his heart, his prayer tonight carried a little
more meaning. He lay in bed a long time, afraid to close his eyes to dream.

About 3:00 a.m. he was wide awake visualizing in every detail the scenes that scared him the most. --He thought about his Mom and Pop, four brothers, and only sister lay sleeping in the rooms next to his own.

Recognizing the security of his family around him, he finally began to relax.----------He was at the point of dozing off when he smelled something like wood burning. He thought that it was his imagination or maybe someone was burning outside in the field, between his house and the street. But then, he reasoned 'why at his time in the morning would anyone be burning anything?' Being the curious fellow that he was, he went out into the hallway to find the answer.

6

That's when he noticed billows
of smoke slowly rising up the
staircase. His first thought was
to wake his mom and pop; they
would know what to do.
When they heard his cry they
awoke with a look of
bewilderment because they
recognized the panic in Billy's
voice. Immediately they smelled
the smoke. Meanwhile, Billy
woke up his brothers and
sisters.
When his parents knew
everyone had been alerted they
led the way down the staircase;

7

after instructing everyone to
hold their breath, not to inhale
the smoke until they were safely
outside. When everyone was
outside, their attention was
drawn to the loud sirens
and roaring of the fire engines
coming to put out the fire.

One of the neighbors was
raiding their icebox early that
morning and was drawn to his
living room window by the
unexplainable
red glare that reflected on the
windowpane. When he
discovered the house was on

8

fire he called the fire
department. While everyone's'
attention was fixed on the
charging red horses, Billy's
youngest brother John (who
was six years old), had ran back
into the house unnoticed to get
his teddy bear. He had
dropped it at the base of the
staircase in his rush to get out
of the house. Billy's family had
ran out of the house in their
pajamas and they would have
virtually frozen to death in that
cold winter night air, but the
neighbors had alerted one

9

another and brought to the
scene with them coats, blankets,
and shoes. That's when Billy's
family realized that John was
missing.
Billy could hear his mother
screaming,
as he ran toward the burning
house. "Where's my little John,
..John!",
He opened the front door and
the flames leaped out at him.
He yelled at the top of his
voice, "Johnny! Johnny!" He
thought he heard a distant cry
coming from the other end of he
building.

10

There was no way he could get through that front door, but somehow he had to save his brother.

Then he remembered the basement window at the back of the house, he was just small enough to fit through. He had opened it the other day and had forgotten to lock it.

The firemen had connected the hoses to the fire hydrant and begun spraying water into the house through the windows. ---Billy's mother was hysterical by now. She was being attended to by the paramedics. Billy's father had seen Billy running behind the house. He took off in pursuit with two firemen close behind. By the time they reached the rear basement window, Billy was already inside. Billy had found his little brother crawling down the cellar stairs clutching his little teddy bear in one hand and trying to keep the smoke from his eyes and nose with the other. He was on the brink of unconsciousness when Billy reached him. Billy picked

John up and carried him toward
the small cellar window where he
found the fireman waiting with
out-stretched arms to receive
John-John through the window.
Then Billy's father helped him
to the .ground
The paramedics were already
feeding John-John pure
oxygen while his father openly
thanked God for this miracle.
Now that his little brother was
safe he felt very tired.

13

He hadn't realized the tremendous pressure his physical and mental being was under. When Billy's mother heard that her baby was safe she stood up and cast her eyes to the heavens. She uttered not a sound as her lips moved and tears streamed down her pale cheeks.

Billy was an outgoing likeable young black boy who would be fourteen his next birthday. The neighborhood was integrated with Italians and blacks.

People who in times of trouble showed a sincere concern toward one another.

At one time or another, Billy had played with some of their children ... gone to school with others. His mom and pop were friendly with everyone.

When tragedy struck, the neighbors came together and responded as one big neighborhood family. They needed a place to stay just for the night. All of their in-laws lived miles and miles away from them.

15

When informed of the tragedy, they began making preparation to pick them up later on that day. Unknown to Billy, the neighbors had gotten together and decided that each household (four in all) would take two people until Billy's relatives arrived.

There was enough excitement that day to last for a lifetime, unexcelled award of a lifetime. For no apparent reason, he began thinking about the day he vowed when he came of age he would join the armed services to fight for his country.

16

The Retreat

To day he feels the need to
communicate within himself.
...... These questions crowded
his mind: *Where have I been?...*
Where am I now?, and ...
Where am I going?
Pondering these things, at the
top of a mountain, isolated from
most of the world.
There is nothing around him
other than his wife, the sound of
the music he loves and seemingly
endless woodlands.
The peace and quiet is what
many of us dream about..

17

While observing and enjoying the surroundings, he could hear nature's song of praise. The rustling of the tree leaves, the call of the wild are exciting sounds in the comfort of the cabin.

There was a longing in his heart that's hard to describe. It is like wanting to hear from a long lost friend, ...like a thirst that can never be quenched. If he could talk to the animals, he would want to know, in every detail, how God provides for them.

18

He wonders if like nature's creatures, he was fulfilling the role in life that God had given him. If he could talk to the animals he would tell them how the Lord has blessed him a human ...down through the years. While looking back, he sees a young black man frightened of the outside world filled with life's uncertainties, raised in an atmosphere ruled by gambling, drinking, and the riotous type of life that follows. He sees a young man fighting against a life

19

he abhorred and as a result grew into manhood at an early age. To take control of his own life, seemed like the only solution to cope with his situation.

He was a young man who needed much encouragement with little to be found. He was trying to make it the best he could. He set his own standards to live by; his own goals to pursue.

During his journey through many mistakes, misconceptions, and searching the mind for answers.

His idealistic ways of thinking made it difficult to conform to a realistic world. He felt as though he belonged to some other world in a different time zone that had passed or was yet to come. There were questions that needed answers. He talked with the young, listened to those with great experience...

The more answers given, the more questions asked, leaving a thirst for understanding, that could not be quenched. Knowing that he would one day marry, he tried to create a vision of his wife to be, ..

21

but only saw a blank face. One day, he walked the streets of the city he knew well. It was where he was born... where his struggle with life had begun. This is where he played ... went to school, and grew up to become a man.

It was one of those cool, crisp mornings, when you step lively to keep warm, and your breathing makes you look like a common smoke stack. His mind was not on the weather as he thought within himself, where he might find people that fit

his mind's image, and how much
better life could be.
Recalling how a business
venture that from all indications
could have been successful, but
turned sour, when his trusted
partner Joseph Signey began
to experiment with his new
passion... women, which
consumed all his time. As he
moved closer to having his
dream come true, he recalled the
day he broke up the
partnership. ------Being a mild
mannered person, he did not get
excited or hysterical,

23

but calmly expressed his desire
to discontinue the partnership.
The results of the breakup left
him with the option to go into
business on his own, ... which he
did. Home life unstable.
Starting a new he realized his
need for salvation. He stopped
walking long enough to close his
eyes, ...look up toward heaven,
and ask God for a new
direction for the rest of his life.

***

The Watermelon
Patch

You know how it
is during those hot
         summer days--
   When many of your friends
      have gone to camp.

   Pedro and his two friends
         stayed home,
   Those very hot and boring
             days,
And there was actually nothing
             to do.
   Two young men, Leroy and
             John

25

Discovered something that
would bring them
a little excitement
As long as they didn't
get caught.
In the courtyard they were
discussing a plan of action when
Pedro walked up on them
unawares.
"What are you guys up to?"
questioned Pedro.
"Oh nothing you would be
interested in?, answered Leroy.
"That's right" John answered
cautiously. But, Pedro
persisted in wanting to know

why they were secretive.
John and Leroy reluctantly
told Pedro about the
watermelon patch they had
discovered and planning to
enjoy the fruit of their
discovery.
Pedro asked, "Where is the
watermelon patch?"
John and Leroy refused to
answer other than to say,
"We know where it is."
The next day, early in the
morning, while the dew drops
lingered on the grass,
they were up and out, on their
way to the watermelon patch.

27

As they approached the train yard, Pedro hadn't figured out yet where the melons were coming from. Pedro walked at a distance, slowly, behind them while they hurriedly walked toward a freight car standing in the freight yard by itself. John broke the lock with a hammer he had hid in his pocket. They opened the door wide enough to enter. Inside, when they could get a better view, they saw long watermelons, short watermelons, fat watermelons. 'What a bonanza', Pedro thought to himself.

28

John and Leroy climbed
inside the freight car and picked
two of the biggest,
ripest watermelons they could
find and headed for the top of
the hill,
to sit on the logs they had
placed there 2 months ago.
Pedro wanted to take a
watermelon but was torn
between the right and wrong of
it. Empty handed,
Pedro ran also to the top of the
hill. He watched them eat those
stolen watermelons with sheer
delight, they tasted so good.

29

They were slurping the juice, and spitting seeds every where. Soon they shared their goodies with Pedro. They were all so busy eating that they were totally unaware of the two men walking up behind them. The men were standing behind them at least 5 minutes before John noticed two shadows protruding beyond their own. John turned around quickly to identify the intruders. Much to their surprise, they were two stern looking, no-nonsense, Officers-of-the-law.

When Pedro and Leroy saw them they almost fell off the log. The Officers introduced themselves as Officer Rodriguez and Officer Hines. Rodriguez began talking. We passed right by you a while ago. We thought it quite unusual to see three young black boys eating watermelon this early in the morning in the train station yard. So, we decided to check it out. "Now fellas", Officer Hines interrupted, "Where did you get these watermelons from?"

Each one of the boys looked at each other as if to say, I wont tell if you don't. Seeing that no one would voluntarily answer that question, Officer Hines asked another question. "Who broke the lock?"

one around him. For in his minds eye, he could see himself handcuffed and on the way to jail. Leroy, on the other hand, could see all his friends laughing and pointing their fingers at him, so John lost sight on the question and everything "jail bird. Jail bird".

32

Pedro felt from the beginning
that it was wrong to break into
the freight cars, so he didn't
break in and he didn't agree with
them, so he didn't take a
watermelon. But, he had
certainly gobbled down a share
of the stolen goods. Pedro
found the courage to answer
the first question. "These
watermelon came from the
freight car", he said; pointing to
the freight car with the broken
lock.
"Well" said Officer Rodriquez,
"do the rest of you have
anything to say?"

33

John shamefully confessed he
had broken the lock. Both
officers congratulated them for
telling the truth and assured
them that this act of courage to
confess the truth would be
considered in their forth coming
punishment. Much to the boys
surprise, the officers asked
them what kind of punishment
did they think would fit their
mischievous deed?
Pedro then asked if they, the
boys, could discuss their answer
in private.

"Be my guest", answered
Officer Rodriguez.
They walked about ten feet
away from the officers and
began their pow-wow.
When their discussion was
concluded about five minutes
later, they walked back to the
officers and Pedro acting as
spokesman, told them they
would work for the rest of the
summer, if necessary, to pay for
the watermelons and damage to
the lock. But they did not want
their parents to know what they
had done.

35

Before answering their request, the officers took their names, ages, and address. Leroy was eleven years old.
John was eleven years old , and Pedro was 12 years old. After taking the names and addresses of their parents, the officers were ready to give an answer to the request.

Officer Hines looked them straight in the eyes and began to speak.
"Now fellas, we must speak with your parents.

They are responsible for you
and many of the things
you may do. I'm sure they will
agree to you taking
responsibility for your actions,
and allow you to work through
the summer
to pay for these damages. I bet
you all will have some money left
over for yourselves." "Thank
you officers" they all said
together.

_____

Ghost of the Past

Ghost of the
    past,
How they linger.
        Blood to blood,
            gene to gene.
    Filtering through generations,
        since the first natural birth
                eons ago.
    The spirit of Aunt Elizabeth
            clothed in flesh,
        through the seed, mannerisms,
            so carefully preserved.
        Hannibal is not dead,
    Though the dust has claimed his
                flesh.
    Some strive with patience to obtain
            the lofty heights.

Others choose the path of infamy,
Some do very little of nothing to
justify their existence,
'Run me off another million copies',
I heard off in the distance.
After careful scrutiny I understood
the patterns was different but the
same.
The incarnate virtues and virtue less
nature of mankind,
Answering countless curtain calls
upon this earthly, domain,
Like the thief with a thousand faces
and portrayals.
Ghosts of the past,...how they
linger,
How they are ever anchored in our
souls.

———————————

39

The Sit Up

Follow the harried hustle and bustle,
Around the bend, to the old dirt
road,
Over the tracks beneath the
trusses,
Where the cluster of vehicles abode.

The old front door of the little
house is creaking,
As people enter in,
The family take turns remorsely
speaking in the crowded den.

Delicious foods, in eating spots are
here ... there... about.
Sitting therein are many stern faces,

A loud TV and minds filled with
doubt.
Greetings are friendly and hearty,
Remember we are to weep at the
coming in.
The voices and laughter... sounds
like a party.
And rejoice at the going out ...
including our kin.

When a love one's gone,
The winner claims the soul.
Never again to roam this earth or
hear their natural voice.
Now the soul can be lost,
whether young of old.
Choose ye this day whom you will
serve, ...your choice.

41

Root of Success

One Spring he chose to plant an
oak tree,
In between the pine and the maple.

When summer breezes began to
cool,
Like the seasons bring
While changing from summer and fall
to winter.

His tree had gone,
From scrawny and peeling
To dropping leaves before time.
Now a skeleton, a dead tree he
thought.

42

Demise, so it appeared, was
merciful.
After standing there all winter,

Spring brings life to it again,
An unpredicted, unexpected,
eliminate resurrection.

Slow growth cursed its very
existence. This time, ...
Rotating blades,
Became its executioner.

Spring came around again,
Growing now after the dormant
season,
More healthy than ever before,
The tree, ...it shall live,
The root is alive.

———————————

You Asked For It

(a retiree's woes)

Steeped in
misery, because no one called,
Why doesn't someone call?
The phone rings all day long,
....But not for him.
Dear Lord, please send a voice over
the phone,
That wants to talk to me.
They do not call me.
I wonder why?
Maybe the Lord heard his prayer.
The first voice on the phone for him
wanted to borrow some money,
How did they know he was a soft
touch.

44

The next phone call for him went like this: "Are you able to take me to Savannah?" That was 45 miles one way.

For one whole month the calls came in; Monday - run me to town please!
Tuesday - could you take me to the doctor.
Wednesday - could you take me to the station?
...And so it continued on.
One day a special friend called...
he spent the entire conversation correcting any word said that might have sounded out of context of our conversation.
The lesson learned, ...watch what you ask for.

45

The Unsung Kloth

While squinting at the shadows,
Through the early morning haze,
I gazed.
Choking the knob on my closet
door,
It taunts me, it beckons me,
To explore, not to ignore,
It's life of servitude.

Listen, the cloth speaks:

Can't use the word humble;
In the explanation of my life;
Cause I cannot make choices;
Or give advice; I'm chosen:

To wash the little children, coming
from play,
To clean the floors, after they are
walked on; ---To even clean the
racks that holds the songs;
To dress all women, boys, girls, and
men too, ---And, ... also shine the
famous leather shoe.
To wash the dirty dishes every day,
To wipe the spills, that all human
makes;
to clean all tools even the iron rake,
To wipe the surface where dust
mites grow, Surely, I must have
polished your   ra-di-o;
I will not name all the things I do,
But in all of this earth,
I'm here to serve you

No Need for Change

New to the south and its southern
ways,
One day I drove half the morning
trying to locate the National Guard
Armory.
"Hi mam, where's the Armory?"
"I need to check with them about a
toys for tots program."
"right there in front of your nose,
...see (pointing).
An elderly gentleman sitting in the
front passenger seat of my car
remarks, "yes, she's right. I use to
come here myself." This southern
gentleman incidentally has been with
me since I started on this journey.

I looked as hard as I could but all I
saw was a vacant vandalized building,
with a boy and girl gym class in
progress.
I parked my car and walked in on the
children playing but could not get
the teachers attention to ask him the
question. After that frustrating
incident, I got back in my car and
drove further down the road, but
ended up at a dead end. I drove
back
to the abandoned building, they
called the Armory but this time I
noticed a gray door that was intact,
so I turned the knob and went in.
Inside was an unkempt officer with
an elderly lady sitting at what looked
like a desk.

49

In a frustrated tone, I asked where is the Armory? She looked puzzled for a moment then her eyes lit up and she replied, "Oh, you mean the 'new' Armory. After I was on my way, as directed, I told the elderly gentleman,

sitting next to me, what I had been told. He replied, "Oh, I know where that is." Out of frustration, I cried out, "Please Lord give me strength to get through this day!"

————————————

From Purpose to Eternity

Death is not generally called our
friend
Years of loss dissipates loneliness
and longing,
Memories drift away like smoke on a
calm summer day,
The heart is challenged by a
formidable opponent.
Stress is defended through prayer.
While childhood proceeds into
productive years.
We hide thoughts of death in a
corner of our mind.
Life's expectancies, uncertainties
and its rewards fill your thoughts,
day after day,

Oft time wonder, what does the
future hold?
Will you be a doctor, lawyer, teacher
or mayor or pastor?
Was told "you can be whatever you
want to be"
My thoughts said, "this is not
logical".
Through prayer, fasting, and
reading the Bible,
A better understanding clarified,
what the saying was saying.

A person's purpose is decided
before birth. Our reason for
existence is shown through our
natural abilities. Allow your natural
gift to guide you to accomplish more
than you think you can.

This is always more rewarding than
the quest for worldly success.

Why am I here is the question? If
you listen to the urging of your gut,
Purpose will take you where you
belong.
Before birth, God has a purpose
for your lives, and we really shine
where we are planted.

If life allow you longevity,
Old age will be your partner.
Everyone is appointed a time to die,
Before you are born, the call is
upon you.
You can't run, you can't hide, or
bargain your way.

53

Many shall lose the battle with
death,
But salvation is everyone's
champion,
It brings with it, everlasting life.
Our Lord and Savior has defeated
death,
And he beckons to you, ...to
celebrate the victory.
The battle cry 'repent' is heard over
and over again.
Hell is a place for the un-repented
souls,
They walk on fire and brimstone
forever.
Heaven is a place for the repented
souls,
They walk on streets of gold
forever.

Positive Thinking Speaks Success

(The tongue... both blesser and curser)

The life you live is what you make it
Divers opportunity abound,
Should you dare to take it.

When faith works, don't know his
grace,
Empty days, empty years,
Follow all tomorrows
Time floats by like a pregnant cloud.
Persistent trials shed sorrow.
Negative thoughts are taken
captive,
Like images in the mirror.

55

The imagination dictates,
The fruit of your labor.

Dreams imitate your thoughts,
Transform your heart, accept the
light.
Drown that sorrow, the forgetful
sea awaits,
Scurry, hurry from that site,
..repent!
Rebuke the shackle, the band that
holds you,
Negative thoughts create strife.
Awaken inherent control of your
earthy pilgrimage.
Authority says, the tongue will
control your life.

Energize new and good thoughts,

56

Eulogize the negative.
Resurrect the positive
Allow the light of salvation to shine
in and upon you.

————————————

The Iniquitous Plan

One lazy afternoon, about mid-
June,
Sat John, humming his favorite
tune,
There's no meal, tasted finer,
Than the food at Richard's diner.

Meanwhile, in walks a young white
man,
His eyes roaming, ...the ominous
scan,

He looks for the one, ...whom he
might,
Force to a heinous fight.
His stinging words carries no tact.
He asks, ...why are you so black?

With a smirk on his face quite bold.,
His questions come bitter and cold.
No word for word, did fall.
Insults parted the air like a fast
pitcher's ball.
But he finally gave up trying,
His trick, the black man, was not
buying.
He finally met a man, that would not
fight.
Tho, he had pushed him, to get up
tight,
But this man's calm reaction
destroyed his
evil plight,
And yes, he was an angel of light.

The Lamp

During the light of day
Sleep rules the dormant ray.
We come alive when you need,
To keep dark shadows at bay.

No! A vampire, God forbid!
Will never fit that slot,
That we are not.
Through the ages wherever we
shine,
An angel of light is more our kind.

Setting among the furniture crowd,
We all are so proud
That one will resist our presence,
Because we shine like the sun's true
essence.

No matter, their form or the shape,
He would want to know about the
cruel, the harsh, the good times they
have endured through the centuries.
Beauty queens, the cameras all
take,
No matter what model they make
Our smile is like a shimmering
crystal clear lake.
When heart failure strikes, oh what a
terrible fright.
The cry, get a light bulb; is out of
sight
Our absence blends into the
darkest night,
But our presence brings no fear,
but light.

Do You Love Me?

In the middle of
My dreams, the hearts
So full, it aching
Your look, your touch
Your lovely smile
I feel my body shaking
Do you love me
As I love you
When I look into your eyes,
Your word is mine
When I take you in my arms,
The feeling is sublime
Do you want me
As I want you,
When I kiss
Your taunting lips

Tender words embrace me
While we hold each other close,
With drawn doubting, links the
My pleading heart cries,
Do not forsake me.
Do you love me,
As I love you?
Do you want me
Like I want you?
Do you love me As I love you?

——————————————

Love Lost

Where love flowed like a river
Emptiness embraces pain.
Misery cuts through the heart
Wielding a knife with a razor's edge.
tomorrows
Like a new cloth to patch a worn
garment
Then death, the burial, the bitter
tears,
Wrought from a love lost.

The inner being cries out, alone
again
The question, "why?" torments the
soul,

She Wore Lavender

I couldn't understand why men act
the fool over some women.
What was it about Cleopatra?
Wake up King Solomon share your
wisdom.
Romeo, tell me something about
Juliet...
Then one day,
Carolyn Aiken wore a lavender
dress
Her black hair draped down,
Each side of her smooth brown skin
face, ...eyes like bambi, the doe.
Beautiful, an ancient clone
appeared.
Her soft quiet manner enhanced her
mystery.

Mesmerized by this beauty
My heart rejoiced and I understood.

————————————

Reborn

While frozen snowflakes
Spread over the barren ground
It uncrystalizes when touched
By the fiery heat waves,
Anxious to dissolve the solid form
Into glistening drops like dew.
As the cold air recedes and if time
shall permit,
A repetitious cold day break,
The winter ice is born again.

——————————

Trifling

Did it ever dawn on you,
What some men do not know
Man came to earth to work,
And follow the guiding light.

No one ever told him, John,
That love carries a responsibility,
If man could live on love alone
Earth would be unlike heaven.

If you do not know the
Basics of life and living,
Experience will open wide
The window to view its
consequences.
You must work for a living
That's what I was taught

Then I met John
Who lives on pure love and emotion.

"It takes two to tango"
So the saying goes
John found a woman who believes in
him as is,
And one day they might marry.

To live this life style... tho
You need, a crutch, an enabler.
Come on mama, step up to the plate
This job! No on else will carry
This story will end here, but
It serves a definite conclusion
This trifling man lives a life
Full of false illusions
It won't work
Man! Get a job!

Root of Success

One Spring he chose
To plant an oak tree,
In between the pine
And the maple.

When the Summer breezes cool
The autumn leaves begin
To display their array of colors,
And the yawning vegetation, are
soon asleep.

The tree, deteriorated from
Scrawny and peeling to
Dropping her leaves before time
"skeleton image," dead tree, he
thought.

Demise, so it appeared, was merciful
Standing lifeless all winter.
Seasons evolve to Spring again,
and
An unpredicted, supposed
resurrection occurs.

Slow growth, loss of patience,
cursed
Its very existence,
Rotating blades
Became the executioner.

Seasons evolve again to Spring.
The tree lives through the dormant
season.
Now more healthy than before,
The tree, it shall live, the root is
alive.

The Hidden Agenda

Inherent void? Dredge the mind!!
Deep compelling thoughts do rest
rain
The souls desire to announce, too
soon,
An anointed idea. While pent-up
creative sites
Bear thought patterns, that look
like forth of July bursts.
This interim digestive period before
expulsion
Holds desire to excel, that creative
thrust
Where planted, grow ideas to help
mankind's
Struggle to break through barriers
to lift his humble existence.

72

Strength of the muck and mire
overwhelms.
The mighty grip against deliverance
must be broken. The contamination,
life's vicissitudes
Lay within thy breast, where the
heart beats
Strive to commit wholly, ye over
comers.
Possible defeat, concerns weigh
heavily,
Stagnating the gift for a season.
The journey's end signals the
exchange
Hope, success, the bounty hunters,
to the rescue.
The mighty voice of triumph, is loud,
clear

73

The winds of adversity cease
clamoring
The hour of rejection, no longer a
threat
Ideas flow freely from inspiration's
fierce eruptions.
They spring forth like the April
showers.
Dormant ideas have surfaced
Vision captured, future assured
Intrinsic treasure, God devised
The hidden agenda is birthed.209

Spirits of the Past

Spirits of the past how they linger
Blood is blood,
Gene to gene,
Filtering through generations
Since the first natural Birth eons
ago,
The virtues and virtue less nature of
Mankind answering countless
curtain calls upon this earthly stage
One man with a thousand faces and
portrayals.
Ghosts of the past, how they linger
How they are ever settled in our
souls.

——————————————

The Good Ole Days
of Pearly

Today I met an elderly negro woman
She had a scrawny appearance
Her legs excessively bowed.
She spoke with a raspy voice
Oft times her words was
indistinguishable as
She related an encounter she once
had.
I was mean ... Wouldn't take nutin
from
When gits angry I feel no pain.
She stared at me with those cold
beady eyes, ...As she continued in
a highly excitable tone, ---While
reliving a past experience.

76

When I was young, she continued,
you'd have to fight me to the end,
I got possessed.   ....I hav ta be
careful nobody devil me up.
Don't wanna go back to that spirit.
I beat ya down to da ground and
never git back.   ---One time my
husband, she chuckled, walked up to
me and pretended as kissing me
....He cut my arm and I didn't know it
Til somebody told me I was
bleeding.
I ran in da house, picked up da iron
You know dose thing for da fire
slipped it up under my coat sleeve,
When I done caught up wid him
I hit him over the haid as hard as I
could, the blood shot out his haid
like a fountain of water.

He fell and got up and start running
out to the street and stopped da
traffic on the main highway
I laughed the whole time,
But we got back together.

————————————————————

Adolescent Dilemma

The sower's seed was planted
within the fertile valley
Of God's last creation.
A mother's travail via love
A father's pain-less delight
Nurturing growth and stature.
A gift to bud and bloom
But as the awkward years unfold,
Dreams are about tomorrow,
Questions need answers.
Aspirations, hope, and imaginations
abound,
Shifting ideas to find purpose.
A niche of stability to self rely,
Assailing most problems

From an infant view.

A visionaries guiding light.
The gap is set to widen.
A generation pregnant with
confusion,
Weaker, wiser but inexperienced
Voids many claims to knowledge,
assumed
Self preservation cancels common
sense.
A cry for help to cross over this time
zone,
To the world on the other side is
heeded-
But this journey must run its course,
For to embrace accountability
Seems a lonely adventure.

Don't Hug Me

If your hug lasts
A nano second
Don't hug me.

If you must grab me
Like a falling log of wood
Don't hug me.

If you have to
Look around
to see who's watching
Don't hug me.

If your hug
Is not from the heart

Don't hug me
If your husband
Is jealous,
Please don't hug me.

If you don't hug
Your husband,
Don't hug me.

———————

A Word to the Wise
is Sufficient

This morning the rain dropped
softly at my door step,
In a hushed voice
They spoke of the wisdom of their
years.
They spoke of purpose, journeys,
and time.
They had been around since the
beginning,
Unspoken and then spoken into
existence.
They told me that life was full of
trouble and strife,
That the same God that spoke
them into existence,

Breathed into man's nostrils and he
became a living soul.
The same God gave them (the rain)
a purpose without free will.
But gave man a purpose and a free
will.
They told me how they envied man
kind,
because he enjoy this privilege..
They couldn't.
After a long silence,
The rain began to praise the
creator
That they were not as man,
Because their desire to fulfill his
purpose never wavered.
Their relationship to God shall
remain the same, as in their
beginning.

But your kind, the raindrops
continued,
Through disobedience... because
you can choose,
Are getting further and further
Away from God's purpose for your
lives.
How sad,
For we know of the treasure
God has in store for you.
If you would only obey His Word.

––––––––––––––––––––

The Poem

Words permeate the mind like
particles of dust, ...Floating, aged
beyond man and creation, waiting to
be recognized, taken, and placed.
The creator through the poet
shapes the body until the poem is
completely formed.
The poem like God's instruments..
Comes to life.
Some with greater anointing than
others, when verbally expressed
through the author.
The personality, the emotional
mood present when the body was
formed,
Is inherent quality,
On constant recall.

A royal family ensues, destined to
mediocrity, fame or somewhere
betwixt.
The poet desires each child its
début... a time to express their
individuality and significance. When
any of the children appear
neglected, his soul (the poet) is
troubled to appease his inspired
work.
Let the dreamer dream,
and help mold some positive realities
that meet the people's needs.
Let the realist enlighten you through
a soliloquy on life's crude
awakenings.
Let the satiated ones fantasize
Far from the cry of the realist,
An improbable escape.

Each inspiration has the created
right to be seen or heard in its
lifetime.
Let the hearers raise the praises.

The Big Mind

O' those lack-a-daisical days,
When he could if he would,
But he wouldn't.
So many opportunities to get things
done... to get ahead.
Tomorrow was always soon enough,
To do what needed to be done
today.
The golden years had eased upon
him,
Now he goes to the doctor...
regularly,
About his heart, his eyes, his
digestive system, and whatever else.
Physically it appears he's falling
apart.
Now that he can't, he would if he
could.

89

He sits around all day looking at
What could have, what should have,
And what would have been.
Too late.
What a time to get, ... the big mind.

————————————

The True Measure of a Man

I believe a man reaches his full
Measure and potential,
When he loves God:
When he recognizes
the voice of God.
Allows God to work out the
purpose for his life.
He exercises his given measure of
faith.
He works within the abilities God
has given him.
He allows his will to become God's
will for his life.
And when he fully understands that
prayer in his life is the priority...
When he lives a "God says well
done" life.

_____

How Could I Have Known

When the stars come out tomorrow
Will I hang my head in sorrow.
When I think of what we had
And what it could've been,
But I was young and oh so' foolish
then.
I didn't know,... how could I know.
While the stars danced above you,
My lips confessed I love you.
That's the way it was,
The story is so old.
But I never knew how much
You meant to me.
Now that you've gone,
Now that you're free... my heart..
Now that I'm without you--

There's no joy in my heart anymore.
I can't sleep. I need your arms
around me.
I can't sleep, for the sound of your
voice.
When the stars come our tomorrow
I will hang my head in sorrow,

————————————————————

Michelle

Full of life, full of joy,
Competitive - compulsive - vibrant
And yet so coy.
On her twelfth birthday,
She knew how to cook
Loves school and learning
And reading her book.

Enjoys short travels
And cherish close friends,
Tuned with curiosity
Just easily blends.

She loves basketball, skating,
Baby sitting and soccer,
Likewise cartoons and rugrats,
But wants to be a doctor.

She covets the TV series Chicago.
The doctors and nurses on screen.
Emergency care to the injured
ongoing are vivid love scenes.
When her hair is undone, oh' what a
pity,
But she wants to go back to the
city.
When she looks so grownup and
pretty.
She's quite a bit to be reckoned
When her eyes fill with tears,
She quite a sleepy head and way
ahead of her years.
She's loved, endeared, and
pampered
And never forgets your special
days,
Our most beloved Shelly.. Shelly
Please keep those charming ways.

95

Where Did I Go Wrong

I remember our wedding day...
We repeated our vows,
And said I do.
I worked night and day,
And gave you all my pay.
I thought that made you happy,
I thought you would be true
But something came between us,
You looked so lonely and blue.
I thought our love was perfect,
Where did I go wrong?
I thought our love was perfect,
Like the melody of a song.
Please don't leave me baby
We can see it through...
Please don't leave me baby
I love no one but you.

Why didn't you tell me
When you began to doubt,
I can't imagine life without you baby
We could have worked it out.

But if your mind is set to leave,
Won't you hear my plea
If you don't make it out there
Please come back to me.
I thought our love was perfect
Like the melody of our song,
I thought our love was perfect
Where did I go wrong?

————————————————

It's Who Know You

Old is old
Old is new
In the mind
Of the Southerner's view.
Who's your Ma?
Who's your Pa?
Who's your next of kin?
Come on now...
Spill your guts.
Tell it with affection,
Could be...
You'll make the right connection.

Wishful Thought
(dear Dad)

We thank you for the meal time talks
and discussions we had every day
this year. Your took time out of
your busy schedule to come to our
school activities.

When you had errands to run, you
took turn to take at least one of us
with you. Thank you for
volunteering and participating in our
school activities. We really enjoyed
our trips to the library. We loved
playing football, computer games,
and basketball with you. Remember
those family vacations where no one
could reach us and we had you all to
ourselves?

99

Thank you for all those hugs and
kisses even when we grew older.
Dad you taught us that Mom was a
very important member of our family.
Dad we knew you loved us,
but you said "You know what, I love
you guys". wow! You taught us how
to treat a lady by the way you
treated Mom and our sister.
We learned a valuable lesson in
respect for ourselves, our parents,
our community, and our country,
because, you showed such great
respect for everyone you came in
contact with. Dad you were always
there for us when we needed you.
You are the best!
Love always,
Your Blessed Children.

Forgiven Not Forgotten
(epitome of respect)

He had seen his father drunk, and
heard him physically abusing his
mother. Her screams echoed
through his mind,
Long after the abuse was over.
He trembled as a cold sweat
covered his head,
Whenever his parents began to
argue.
Then came the running, the
screaming,
The house seem to be falling apart.
Dishes, pots, and pans fell from the
cabinets.
Whenever he was alone with his
mother,

He verbally lashed out at his
father's behavior.
Only to be told by his mother,
"He's your father, so hold your
tongue".
"You're not going to disrespect
your father."
At the age of fourteen, he was very
athletic,
Thin in statue, and unusually strong
for his age.
Carrying wood and coal on his back
from the railroad yard,
And toting baskets of wood from
the lumber yard
At least three quarters of a mile,
To his house. All up the hill,
Had made him stronger than he
realized.

He had finally decided he would put a stop to his father's physical abuse of his mother.

The very next time it happened, it was in the upstairs bedroom. From his bedroom, he rushed to the aid of his mother,

Pinned his father against the wall,

————————————————

www.ingramcontent.com/pod-product-compliance
Lightning Source LLC
Chambersburg PA
CBHW070814050426
42452CB00011B/2034